T0082562

Hang
in
There

QUOTES & MEDITATIONS FOR
SPIRITUAL SURVIVAL

JEANETTE BISHOP & HELEN VARGA

authorHOUSE®

AuthorHouse™
1663 Liberty Drive
Bloomington, IN 47403
www.authorhouse.com
Phone: 1 (800) 839-8640

Published by AuthorHouse 03/31/2017

ISBN: 978-1-5246-8478-5 (sc)
ISBN: 978-1-5246-8480-8 (e)

Library of Congress Control Number: 2017904475

Print information available on the last page.

Introduction

This book was guided by Spirit, due to the current underlying spiritual crisis resulting from our societal and global climate. Despite all our knowledge and vast spiritual experiences, we also have doubted God. Various institutions (political, religious, educational, familial and the like) along with the media remind us that we are never good enough, thus devaluing and demoralizing our being and even questioning our soul's intuitiveness.

"Why even bother?" we asked God and Spirit.

With life's seeming uncertainties, we too have felt close to feeling defeated and have turned to Spirit asking for comfort, for guidance.

"Hang in there," Spirit replied.

One never knows when life is about to change for the better; while we cannot see it, Spirit can. Spirit has always reminded us, "Even out of your negative experiences, there comes something positive." With life's turmoil's we often lose hope; we lose faith in God and want to give up on the world including ourselves. We wish this little book filled with the love of God and Spirit to remind you never to give up hope and to never give up on yourself, as love will always find a way.

Even when you don't want to be reminded to have hope, and it's hard as hell – hang in there!

God and Spirit
never give up on us;
we give up on ourselves.

*Divine Intervention happens
when we open our
eyes and hearts to see.*

*Spiritual growth
isn't easy –
it's not just reading
a nice book or quote,
it's about changing
your consciousness
and making it
a part of your
neural network daily.*

Our spiritual light
attracts love –
so shine brightly
and know there is
a far more expansive light
shining on you!

Mantra

*I unburden my soul
from human constructs
by letting go*

*Imagine Spirit saying to you,
"The only love we know is you."*

It is through love
that we manifest our spirituality.

– WTF I'm Trying to Be Spiritual – A Guidebook

*Do not negate
your spiritual progress
with negativity;
you just need to know
every step you take
forward and back
are a spiritual process.*

Being spiritual isn't about being disconnected from the world, it's about experiencing life.

If we stay with what we know,
then we cannot grow.

Whatever you call your
faith or spirituality,
you aren't meant
to live life shackled.

– WTF I'm Trying to Be Spiritual – A Workbook

Our self-hatred and guilt accomplish nothing other than acting as a locked door to any change we may want to make.

Affirmation

*I make up
my own wrath
and punishments
to which God
pours Love over
to show me
love is the only way
through the life
I create, not fear.*

Often we stifle our creativity, and it prevents us from reaching into our soul to the beautiful creator that we are.

The love
you have inside
is deeper than
the universe,
and it is only your
earthbound thinking
that holds you back
from creating.

*By living as best as you can
in the power of love,
you will begin to feel happy
for no reason.*

*Do not assess
your value
based on people
who have no value
in spirit or
a moral compass.*

One's past
does not have to
rule the future
by using
one's past suffering
as the gauge.

Stop martyrdom;
sharing is more conducive to a
healthy mind and body.

– WTF I'm Trying to Be Spiritual – A Guidebook

If you are a creator,
then you can create
whatever you wish,
so wish for love
and happiness,
and choose
well and wisely.

– WTF I'm Trying to Be Spiritual – A Guidebook

Don't let the
ego emotions,
which breed negativity,
tell you what you
deserve.

– WTF I'm Trying to Be Spiritual – A Guidebook

*Create the wonderful,
and start now.*

– WTF I'm Trying to Be Spiritual – A Guidebook

The love angels
give to us
is a reminder
of the love
to give to ourselves
on a daily basis.

What does it cost you to love yourself?

You are beautiful
in your own right,
and loving yourself for
a split second every day
is enough to start
that ripple effect
in your own lives,
in your own being,
and with everybody
that you meet.

– WTF I'm Trying to Be Spiritual – A Guidebook

God considers all beings whole
and wraps Love around
every living thing.

Affirmation

*I am whole,
and I have no need,
nor desire
to block myself
with the power
of self-hatred.*

God accepts us,
regardless of how
we choose to
experience ourselves,
our divinity, higher power,
life force, unconditional love,
soul, spirit, self, intuition,
essence, gut feeling,
or however you deem it.

– WTF I'm Trying to Be Spiritual – A Guidebook

*By witnessing
all the beauty
around you
with your own eyes,
without judgment,
you will see the
divine within you.*

– WTF I'm Trying to Be Spiritual – A Guidebook

In essence, Love is light;
it shines regardless.

– WTF I'm Trying to Be Spiritual – A Guidebook

Mantra

I accept love
on any level I'm able to, today

*Spiritual gifts
are not for
the chosen few –
few choose
to develop them.*

You tap into
the Universal Source
once you are free
from the negative self-talk.

No matter what,
there is a beautiful,
benevolent energy/spirit
that walks with you.

*Asking for
guidance from Spirit
means patience
as you will always
get help;
it may not come
in the way you want
but in the way
that you need.*

Mantra

I stay open to spiritual expansion

Weathering
the storms of life
can be difficult enough
but with Spirit
by your side,
supporting you
with love and intention,
you will get through.

There will always
be horrific events
going on somewhere
in the world,
just focus on being
a loving person
and only allow
love at your door.

*We only have
this life to enjoy
in the present,
and we may
have lived before,
but what is the use
in knowing that,
if we can't even live the
life we have now?*

*You can have a
road map for life,
however,
just remember
that detours
are just another way
which reveals your
soul's plan.*

Without entropy,
transformations
cannot take place.

Do not be afraid of entropy;
it means something is changing
because you want it too!

You are resilient;
it's your thoughts
that tell you otherwise.

*We can all feel stranded
from time to time,
what's important is
not to dwell on it
and look for the route
toward fulfillment.*

Negative experiences only show you how deep your positive experiences can be and vice-versa.

– WTF I'm Trying to Be Spiritual – A Guidebook

Just remember that when things, places, and people fall away, that's only another beginning, a rebirth if you will, into something more conducive to your spiritual growth.

– WTF I'm Trying to Be Spiritual – A Workbook

*You can expect the best
from the universe;
just be careful you do not
put expectations
upon that outcome.
Sometimes you won't
know what is the best
and for whom it
would be the best.*

– WTF I'm Trying to Be Spiritual – A Guidebook

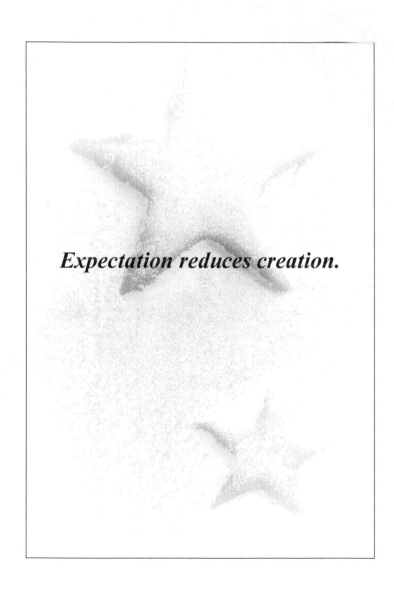

Expectation reduces creation.

*As soon as we
let go of expectations,
then we begin to see
all the little miracles
that happen around us.*

State,
"I've done everything I can.
I am asking for the
highest and the best
in the universe.
It may not be the way
I want it, but it'll be the way
which is best for
everyone concerned."

– WTF I'm Trying to Be Spiritual – A Guidebook

*The universe
doesn't recognize any religion,
just what you ask for.*

*Having the patience
for prayers to be answered
can be difficult –
the time has to be right
for all concerned.*

*Sometimes people are
removed from our lives by
Divine Intervention
for a reason,
don't chase them or
invite them back;
often we don't realize
at the time it was to help us
move forward or take stock.*

*Silver linings are a way
to show us with hindsight
things weren't right anyway.*

Angels are present everywhere,
we just have to open
our minds and hearts
to witness them,
some come in human form,
some as animals but the greatest
angel of all time is our Earth,
the beauty she brings us
is far beyond our ken.

There are so many
angelic happenings
to prove to us
in a myriad of ways that
the Universal Source loves us.

*How can the universe
roll in with gifts
if you keep refusing them?*

*Don't think
of giving up;
think instead
of giving way to the
universe's gifts
by getting out of
your way.*

Our fear of success and failure are linked to superstition and fear.

– WTF I'm Trying to Be Spiritual – A Guidebook

*We have been trained
to think of failure
as a bad thing,
just know it isn't;
it is a learning curve,
resulting in
further learning.*

There is always
a light to direct you,
and sometimes it comes
from unexpected places
rather than the norm!

Affirmation

*I'm where I need to be
at this moment in time;
my soul knows exactly
what it's doing.*

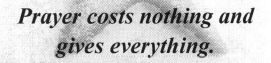

Prayer costs nothing and gives everything.

Every thought is a form of a supplication and is a living energy – change your thoughts to great supplications.

*It's best to let it go
and allow the universe
to lead the way;
its hallways
are always open and lit
for our benefit.*

*If you feel
let down by God
because of
unanswered prayers
then maybe you were
asking for something
which wasn't
in your destiny or
the timing wasn't right.*

*The Universal Source responds
when it's time, showing us
the way and often we
aren't aware until later –
with hindsight!*

We want to have knowing.
Spirit told us,
"If you have knowing,
then prayer is not asking,
it is gratitude."

– WTF I'm Trying to Be Spiritual – A Workbook

Blessing another person
isn't a sign of weakness
– it is a sign of strength,
as you know the universe
will respond kindly.

*Neither God nor Spirit
take sides – there are no
inferior or superior individuals –
there are only human
lessons, love, and growth.*

Mantra

My need for allies diminishes with God

We are all
someone's gift,
maybe for a moment,
a day, a lifetime
– it doesn't matter –
unwrap your
beautiful self
from negativity
and share.

*Being vulnerable means
you can feel and love,
rather than
shut out and ignore.*

– WTF I'm Trying to Be Spiritual – A Guidebook

We all have our
demons, stress of life,
and people who can leave
us feeling bereft of love;
the reality is
love never leaves,
it's always within us,
and often we have to
fight to reveal it.

*Peace within
comes from knowing
that you are following
your moral compass with
love and integrity.*

It's okay to have boundaries;
they keep us sane
in moments of insanity
when we forget we're
worthy of good things.

Practicing self-love
can be hard
however
just put your hand
over your heart
and remember
it's beating for a reason.

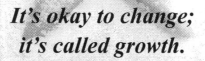

*It's okay to change;
it's called growth.*

You have been led to believe
in your inadequacy.

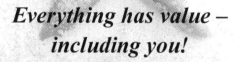

Everything has value –
including you!

*Give yourself
permission to live
a human life,
not a "perfect" life
defined by others.*

– WTF I'm Trying to Be Spiritual – A Guidebook

*You are not
the accumulation of
others' opinions.*

– WTF I'm Trying to Be Spiritual – A Guidebook

You define you.

– WTF I'm Trying to Be Spiritual – A Guidebook

Affirmation

The opinions of others
are not a reflection
of who I am.
Opinions are perceptions,
and I am neither
a perception nor a reflection
of a perception.

God's will for you
is to grow with
love, understanding,
and awareness,
to heal suffering
in mind, body, and spirit.

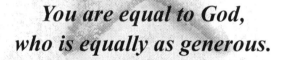

You are equal to God,
who is equally as generous.

God's grace is with all beings regardless of human interpretations.

Affirmation

*I am only limited by
the size of my ocean of love
I see, and by how I perceive
God's unconditional love.
I decide.
I am patient.
I am wise.*

*You can seek and search
within books and the like, but
the real gem is your soul
speaking to you,
trying to guide you to
love, kindness, and joy.*